Book 1
Python Programming Professional Made Easy
BY SAM KEY

&

Book 2
JavaScript Professional Programming Made Easy
BY SAM KEY

Book 1
Python Programming Professional Made Easy

By Sam Key

Expert Python Programming Language Success in a Day for Any Computer User!

Table Of Contents

Introduction

I want to thank you and congratulate you for purchasing the book, "Python Programming Professional Made Easy: Expert Python Programming Language Success in a Day for Any Computer User!"

This book contains proven steps and strategies on how to program Python in a few days. The lessons ingrained here will serve as an introduction to the Python language and programming to you. With the little things you will learn here, you will still be able to create big programs.

The book is also designed to prepare you for advanced Python lessons. Make sure that you take note of all the pointers included here since they will help you a lot in the future.

Thanks again for purchasing this book. I hope you enjoy it!

Chapter 1: Introduction to Programming Languages

This short section is dedicated to complete beginners in programming. Knowing all the things included in this chapter will lessen the confusion that you might encounter while learning Python or any programming language.

Computers do not know or cannot do anything by itself. They just appear smart because of the programs installed on them.

Computer, Binary, or Machine Language

You cannot just tell a computer to do something using human language since they can only understand computer language, which is also called machine or binary language. This language only consists of 0's and 1's.

On the other hand, you may not know how to speak or write computer language. Even if you do, it will take you hours before you can tell a computer to do one thing since just one command may consist of hundreds or thousands of 1's and 0's. If you translate one letter in the human alphabet to them, you will get two or three 1's or 0's in return. Just imagine how many 1's and 0's you will need to memorize if you translate a sentence to computer language.

Assembly or Low Level Programming Language

In order to overcome that language barrier, programmers have developed assemblers. Assemblers act as translators between a human and a computer.

However, assemblers cannot comprehend human language. They can only translate binary language to assembly language and vice versa. So, in order to make use of assemblers, programmers need to learn their language, which is also called a low level language.

Unfortunately, assembly language is difficult to learn and memorize. Assembly language consists of words made from mnemonics that only computer experts know. And for one to just make the computer display something to the screen, a programmer needs to type a lot of those words.

High Level Programming Language

Another solution was developed, and that was high level programming languages such as C++, Java, and Python. High level programming languages act as a translator for humans and assembly language or humans to computer language.

Unlike assembly language (or low level language), high level programming languages are easier to understand since they commonly use English words instead of mnemonics. With it, you can also write shorter lines of codes since they already provide commonly used functions that are shortened into one or two keywords.

If you take one command or method in Python and translate it to assembly language, you will have long lines of codes. If you translate it to computer language, you will have thousands of lines composed of 1's and 0's.

In a nutshell, high level programming languages like Python are just translators for humans and computers to understand each other. In order for computers to do something for humans, they need to talk or instruct them via programming languages.

Many high level languages are available today. Among the rest, Python is one of the easiest languages to learn. In the next chapter, you will learn how to speak and write with Python language for your computer to do your bidding.

Chapter 2: Getting Prepped Up

On the previous chapter, you have learned the purpose of programming languages. By choosing this book, you have already decided that Python is the language that you want to use to make your programs. In this chapter, your learning of speaking, writing, and using this language starts.

You, Python, and Your Computer

Before you start writing, take a moment to understand the relationship between you, the programming language, and the computer. Imagine that you are a restaurant manager, and you have hired two foreign guys to cook for the restaurant, which is the program you want to create. The diners in your restaurant are the users of your program.

The first guy is the chef who only knows one language that you do not know. He follows recipes to the letter, and he does not care if the recipe includes him jumping off the cliff. That guy is your computer.

The second guy is the chef's personal translator who will translate the language you speak or write, which is Python, to the language the chef knows. This translator is strict and does not tolerate typos in the recipes he translates. If he finds any mistake, he will tell it right to your face, walk away with the chef, and leave things undone.

He also does not care if the recipe tells the chef to run on circles until he dies. That is how they work. This guy is your programming language.

Since it is a hassle to tell them the recipe while they cook, you decided to write a recipe book instead. That will be your program's code that the translator will read to the chef.

Installing Python

You got two things to get to program in Python. First, get the latest release of Python. Go to this website: https://www.python.org/downloads/.

Download Python 3.4.2 or anything newer than that. Install it. Take note of the directory where you will install Python.

Once you are done with the installation, you must get a source code editor. It is recommended that you get Notepad++. If you already have a source code editor, no need to install Notepad++, too. To download Notepad++, go to: http://www.notepad-plus-plus.org/download/v6.6.9.html. Download and install it.

Version 2.x or 3.x

If you have already visited the Python website to download the program, you might have seen that there are two Python versions that you can download. As of this writing, the first version is Python 3.4.2 and the second version is Python 2.7.8.

About that, it is best that you get the latest version, which is version 3.4.2. The latest version or build will be the only one getting updates and fixes. The 2.7.8 was already declared as the final release for the 2.x build.

Beginners should not worry about it. It is recommended that new Python programmers start with 3.x or later before thinking about exploring the older versions of Python.

Programming and Interactive Mode

Python has two modes. The first one is Programming and the second one is Interactive. You will be using the Interactive mode for the first few chapters of this book. On the other hand, you will be using the Programming mode on the last few chapters.

In Interactive mode, you can play around with Python. You can enter lines of codes on it, and once you press enter, Python will immediately provide a feedback or execute the code you input. To access Python's interactive mode, go to the directory where you installed Python and open the Python application. If you are running on Windows, just open the Run prompt, enter python, and click OK.

In Programming mode, you can test blocks of code in one go. Use a source editor to write the program. Save it as a .py file, and run it as Python program. In Windows, .py files will be automatically associated with Python after you install Python. Due to that, you can just double click the file, and it will run.

Chapter 3: Statements

A program's code is like a recipe book. A book contains chapters, paragraphs, and sentences. On the other hand, a program's code contains modules, functions, and statements. Modules are like chapters that contain the recipes for a full course meal. Procedures or functions are like paragraphs or sections that contain recipes. Statements are like the sentences or steps in a recipe. To code a program with Python, you must learn how to write statements.

Statements

Statements are the building blocks of your program. Each statement in Python contains one instruction that your computer will follow. In comparison to a sentence, statements are like imperative sentences, which are sentences that are used to issue commands or requests. Unlike sentences, Python, or programming languages in general, has a different syntax or structure.

For example, type the statement below on the interpreter:

print("Test")

Press the enter key. The interpreter will move the cursor to the next line and print 'Test' without the single quotes. The command in the sample statement is print. The next part is the details about the command the computer must do. In the example, it is ("test"). If you convert that to English, it is like you are commanding the computer to print the word Test on the program.

Python has many commands and each of them has unique purpose, syntax, and forms. For example, type this and press enter:

1 + 1

Python will return an answer, which is 2. The command there is the operator plus sign. The interpreter understood that you wanted to add the two values and told the computer to send the result of the operation.

Variables

As with any recipe, ingredients should be always present. In programming, there will be times that you would want to save some data in case you want to use them later in your program. And there is when variables come in.

Variables are data containers. They are the containers for your ingredients. You can place almost any type of data on them like numbers or text. You can change the value contained by a variable anytime. And you can use them anytime as long as you need them.

To create one, all you need is to think of a name or identifier for the variable and assign or place a value to it. To create and assign a value to variables, follow the example below:

example1 = 10

On the left is the variable name. On the right is the value you want to assign to the variable. If you just want to create a variable, you can just assign 0 to the variable to act as a placeholder. In the middle is the assignment operator, which is the equal sign. That operator tells the interpreter that you want him to assign a value, which is on its right, to the name or object on the left.

To check if the variable example1 was created and it stored the value 10 in it, type the variable name on the interpreter and press enter. If you done it correctly, the interpreter will reply with the value of the variable. If not, it will reply with a NameError: name <variable_name> is not defined. It means that no variable with that name was created.

Take note, you cannot just create any name for a variable. You need to follow certain rules to avoid receiving syntax errors when creating them. And they are:

- Variable names should start with an underscore or a letter.
- Variable names must only contain letters, numbers, or underscores.
- Variable names can be one letter long or any length.
- Variable names must not be the same with any commands or reserved keywords in Python.
- Variable names are case sensitive. The variable named example1 is different from the variable named Example1.

As a tip, always use meaningful names for your variables. It will help you remember them easily when you are writing long lines of codes. Also, keep them short and use only one style of naming convention. For example, if you create a variable like thisIsAString make sure that you name your second variable like that too: thisIsTheSecondVariable not this_is_the_second_variable.

You can do a lot of things with variables. You can even assign expressions to them. By the way, expressions are combinations of numbers and/or variables together with operators that can be evaluated by the computer. For example:

Example1 = 10

Example2 = 5 + 19

Example3 = Example1 - Example2

If you check the value of those variables in the interpreter, you will get 10 for Example1, 24 for Example2, and -14 for Example3.

Chapter 4: Basic Operators – Part 1

As of this moment, you have already seen three operators: assignment (=), addition (+), and subtraction (-) operators. You can use operators to process and manipulate the data and variables you have – just like how chefs cut, dice, and mix their ingredients.

Types of Python Operators

Multiple types of operators exist in Python. They are:

- **Arithmetic**
- **Assignment**
- **Comparison**
- **Logical**
- **Membership**
- **Identity**
- **Bitwise**

Up to this point, you have witnessed how arithmetic and assignment operators work. During your first few weeks of programming in Python, you will be also using comparison and logical operators aside from arithmetic and assignment operators. You will mostly use membership, identity, and bitwise later when you already advanced your Python programming skills.

As a reference, below is a list of operators under arithmetic and assignment. In the next chapter, comparison and logical will be listed and discussed briefly in preparation for later lessons.

For the examples that the list will use, x will have a value of 13 and y will have a value of 7.

Arithmetic

Arithmetic operators perform mathematical operations on numbers and variables that have numbers stored on them.

> + : Addition. Adds the values besides the operator.

z = 13 + 7

z's value is equal to 20.

- : Subtraction. Subtracts the values besides the operator.

z = x – y

z's value is equal to 6.

*** : Multiplication. Multiplies the values besides the operator.**

z = x * y

z's value is equal to 91.

/ : Division. Divides the values besides the operator.

z = x / y

z's value is equal to 1.8571428571428572.

**** : Exponent. Applies exponential power to the value to the left (base) with the value to the right (exponent).**

z = x ** y

z's value is equal to 62748517.

// : Floor Division. Divides the values besides the operator and returns a quotient with removed digits after the decimal point.

z = x // y

z's value is equal to 1.

% : Modulus. Divides the values besides the operator and returns the remainder instead of the quotient.

z = x % y

z's value is equal to 6.

Assignment

Aside from the equal sign or simple assignment operator, other assignment operators exist. Mostly, they are combinations of arithmetic operators and the simple assignment operator.

They are used as shorthand methods when reassigning a value to a variable that is also included in the expression that will be assigned to it. Using them in your code simplifies and makes your statements clean.

= : Simple assignment operator. It assigns the value of the expression on its right hand side to the variable to its left hand side.

z = x + y * x – y % x

z's value is equal to 97.

The following assignment operators work like this: it applies the operation first on the value of the variable on its left and the result of the expression on its right. After that, it assigns the result of the operation to the variable on its left.

+= : Add and Assign

x += y

x's value is equal to 20. It is equivalent to x = x + y.

-= : Subtract and Assign

x −= y

x's value is equal to 6. It is equivalent to x = x – y.

*= : Multiply and assign

x *= y

x's value is equal to 91. It is equivalent to x = x * y.

/= : Divide and assign

x /= y

x's value is equal to 1.8571428571428572. It is equivalent to x = x / y.

**= : Exponent and Assign

x **= y

x's value is equal to 62748517. It is equivalent to x = x ** y.

//= : Floor Division and Assign

x //= y

x's value is equal to 1. It is equivalent to x = x // y.

%= : Modulus and Assign

x %= y

x's value is equal to 6. It is equivalent to x = x % y.

Multiple Usage of Some Operators

Also, some operators may behave differently depending on how you use them or what values you use together with them. For example:

z = "sample" + "statement"

As you can see, the statement tried to add two strings. In other programming languages, that kind of statement will return an error since their (+) operator is dedicated for addition of numbers only. In Python, it will perform string concatenation that will append the second string to the first. Hence, the value of variable z will become "samplestatement".

On the other hand, you can use the (-) subtraction operator as unary operators. To denote that a variable or number is negative, you can place the subtraction operator before it. For example:

z = 1 - -1

The result will be 2 since 1 minus negative 1 is 2.

The addition operator acts as a unary operator for other languages; however, it behaves differently in Python. In some language, an expression like this: +(-1), will be treated as positive 1. In Python, it will be treated as +1(-1), and if you evaluate that, you will still get negative 1.

To perform a unary positive, you can do this instead:

--1

In that example, Python will read it as –(-1) or -1 * -1 and it will return a positive 1.

Chapter 5: Basic Operators – Part 2

Operators seem to be such a big topic, right? You will be working with them all the time when programming in Python. Once you master or just memorize them all, your overall programming skills will improve since most programming languages have operators that work just like the ones in Python.

And just like a restaurant manager, you would not want to let your chef serve food with only unprocessed ingredients all the time. Not everybody wants salads for their dinner.

Comparison

Aside from performing arithmetic operations and storing values to variables, Python can also allow you to let the computer compare expressions. For example, you can ask your computer if 10 is greater than 20. Since 10 is greater than 20, it will reply with True – meaning the statement you said was correct. If you have compared 20 is greater than 10 instead, it will return a reply that says False.

== : Is Equal

z = x == y

z's value is equal to FALSE.

!= : Is Not Equal

z = x != y

z's value is equal to True.

> : Is Greater Than

z = x > y

z's value is equal to True.

< : Is Less Than

z = x < y

z's value is equal to FALSE.

>= : Is Greater Than or Equal

z = x >= y

z's value is equal to True.

<= : Is Less Than or Equal

z = x <= y

z's value is equal to FALSE.

Note that the last two operators are unlike the combined arithmetic and simple assignment operator.

Logical

Aside from arithmetic and comparison operations, the computer is capable of logical operations, too. Even simple circuitry can do that, but that is another story to tell.

Anyway, do you remember your logic class where your professor talked about truth tables, premises, and propositions? Your computer can understand all of that. Below are the operators you can use to perform logic in Python. In the examples in the list, a is equal to True and b is equal to False.

and : Logical Conjunction AND. It will return only True both the propositions or variable besides it is True. It will return False if any or both the propositions are False.

w = a and a

x = a and b

y = b and a

z = b and b

w is equal to True, x is equal to False, y is equal to False, and z is equal to False.

or : Logical Disjunction OR. It will return True if any or both of the proposition or variable beside it is True. It will return False if both the propositions are False.

w = a or a

x = a or b

y = b or a

z = b or b

w is equal to True, x is equal to True, y is equal to True, and z is equal to False.

not : Logical Negation NOT. Any Truth value besides it will be negated. If True is negated, the computer will reply with a False. If False is negated, the computer will reply with a True.

w = not a

x = not b

w is equal to False and x is equal to True.

If you want to perform Logical NAND, you can use Logic Negation NOT and Logical Conjunction AND. For example:

w = not (a and a)

x = not (a and b)

y = not (b and a)

z = not (b and b)

w is equal to False, x is equal to True, y is equal to True, and z is equal to True.

If you want to perform Logical NOR, you can use Logic Negation NOT and Logical Disjunction OR. For example:

w = not (a or a)

x = not (a or b)

y = not (b or a)

z = not (b or b)

w is equal to False, x is equal to False, y is equal to False, and z is equal to True.

You can perform other logical operations that do not have Python operators by using conditional statements, which will be discussed later in this book.

Order of Precedence

In case that your statement contains multiple types or instances of operators, Python will evaluate it according to precedence of the operators, which is similar to the PEMDAS rule in Mathematics. It will evaluate the operators with the highest precedence to the lowest. For example:

z = 2 + 10 / 10

Instead of adding 2 and 10 first then dividing the sum by 10, Python will divide 10 by 10 first then add 2 to the quotient instead since division has a higher precedence than subtraction. So, instead of getting 1.2, you will get 3.0. In case that it confuses you, imagine that Python secretly adds parentheses to the expression. The sample above is the same as:

z = 2 + (10 / 10)

If two operators with the same level of precedence exist in one statement, Python will evaluate the first operator that appears from the left. For example:

z = 10 / 10 * 2

The value of variable z will be 2.

Take note that any expressions inside parentheses or nested deeper in parentheses will have higher precedence than those expressions outside the parentheses. For example:

z = 2 / ((1 + 1) * (2 – 4))

Even though the division operator came first and has higher precedence than addition and subtraction, Python evaluated the ones inside the parentheses first and evaluated the division operation last. So, it added 1 and 1, subtracted 4 from 2, multiplied the sum and difference of the two previous operations, and then divided the product from 2. The value of variable z became -0.5.

Below is a reference for the precedence of the operations. The list is sorted from operations with high precedence to operators with low precedence.

- **Exponents**
- **Unary**
- **Multiplication, Division, Modulo, and Floor Division**
- **Addition, and Subtraction**
- **Bitwise**
- **Comparison**
- **Assignment**
- **Identity**
- **Membership**
- **Logical**

Truth Values

The values True and False are called truth values – or sometimes called Boolean data values. The value True is equal to 1 and the value False is equal to 0. That means that you can treat or use 1 as the truth value True and 0 as the truth value False. Try comparing those two values in your interpreter. Code the following:

True == 1

False == 0

The interpreter will return a value of True – meaning, you can interchange them in case a situation arises. However, it is advisable that that you use them like that sparingly.

Another thing you should remember is that the value True and False are case sensitive. True != TRUE or False != false. Aside from that, True and False are Python keywords. You cannot create variables named after them.

You might be wondering about the use of truth values in programming. The answer is, you can use them to control your programs using conditional or flow control tools. With them, you can make your program execute statements when a certain condition arises. And that will be discussed on the next chapter.

Chapter 6: Functions, Flow Control, and User Input

With statements, you have learned to tell instructions to the computer using Pythons. As of now, all you know is how to assign variables and manipulate expressions. And the only command you know is print. Do you think you can make a decent program with those alone? Maybe, but you do not need to rack your brains thinking of one.

In this chapter, you will learn about functions and flow control. This time, you will need to leave the interpreter or Interactive mode. Open your source code editor since you will be programming blocks of codes during this section.

Functions

Statements are like sentences in a book or steps in a recipe. On the other hand, functions are like paragraphs or a recipe in a recipe book. Functions are blocks of code with multiple statements that will perform a specific goal or goals when executed. Below is an example:

```
def recipe1():

    print("Fried Fish Recipe")

    print("Ingredients:")

    print("Fish")

    print("Salt")

    print("Steps:")

    print("1. Rub salt on fish.")

    print("2. Fry fish.")

    print("3. Serve.")
```

The function's purpose is to print the recipe for Fried Fish. To create a function, you will need to type the keyword def (for define) then the name of the function. In the example, the name of the function is recipe1. The parentheses are important to be present there. It has its purpose, but for now, leave it alone.

After the parentheses, a colon was placed. The colon signifies that a code block will be under the function.

To include statements inside that code block, you must indent it. In the example, one indentation or tab was used. To prevent encountering errors, make sure that all the statements are aligned and have the same number of indentations.

To end the code block for the function, all you need is to type a statement that has the same indentation level of the function declaration.

By the way, all the statements inside a function code block will not be executed until the function is called or invoked. To invoke the function, all you need is to call it using its name. To invoke the function recipe1, type this:

```
recipe1()
```

And that is how simple functions work.

Flow Control

It is sad that only one recipe can be displayed by the sample function. It would be great if your program can display more recipes. And letting the user choose the recipe that they want to be displayed on the program would be cool. But how can you do that?

You can do that by using flow control tools in Python. With them, you can direct your program to do something if certain conditions are met. In the case of the recipe listing program, you can apply flow control and let them see the recipes by requesting it.

If Statement

The simplest control flow tool you can use for this type of project is the if statement. Have you been wondering about truth values? Now, you can use them with if statements.

An *if statement* is like a program roadblock. If the current condition of your program satisfies its requirements, then it will let it access the block of statements within it. It is like a function with no names, and instead of being invoked to work, it needs you to satisfy the conditions set to it. For example:

```
a = 2

if a == 2:

        print("You satisfied the condition!")

        print("This is another statement that will be executed!")

if a == (1 + 1):

        print("You satisfied the condition again!")

        print("I will display the recipe for Fried Fish!")

        recipe1()
```

If you will translate the first if statement in English, it will mean that: if variable a is equals to 2, then print the sentence inside the parentheses. Another way to translate it is: if the comparison between variable a and the number 2 returns True, then print the sentence inside the parentheses.

As you can see, the colon is there and the statements below the if statement are indented, too. It really is like a function.

User Input

You can now control the flow of your program and create functions. Now, about the recipe program, how can the user choose the recipe he wants to view? That can be done by using the input() command. You can use it like this:

a = input("Type your choice here and press enter: ")

Once Python executes that line, it will stop executing statements. And provide a prompt that says "Type your choice here: ". During that moment, the user will be given a chance to type something in the program. If the user press enter, Python will store and assign the characters the user typed on the program to variable a. Once that process is done, Python will resume executing the statements after the input statement.

In some cases, programmers use the input command to pause the program and wait for the user to press enter. You can do that by just placing input() on a line.

With that, you can make a program that can capture user input and can change its flow whenever it gets the right values from the user. You can create a recipe program that allows users to choose the recipe they want. Here is the code. Analyze it. And use the things you have learned to improve it. Good luck.

```
print("Enter the number of the recipe you want to read.")

print("1 - Fried Fish")

print("2 - Fried Egg")

print("Enter any character to Exit")

choice = input("Type a Number and Press Enter: ")


if choice == "1":

    print("Fried Fish Recipe")

    print("Ingredients:")

    print("Fish")
```

```
    print("Salt")
    print("Steps:")
    print("1. Rub salt on fish.")
    print("2. Fry fish.")
    print("3. Serve.")
    pause = input("Press enter when you are done reading.")

if choice == "2":
    print("Fried Egg Recipe")
    print("Ingredients:")
    print("Egg")
    print("Salt")
    print("Steps:")
    print("1. Fry egg.")
    print("2. Sprinkle Salt.")
    print("3. Serve.")
    pause = input("Press enter when you are done reading.")
```

Conclusion

Thank you again for purchasing this book!

I hope this book was able to help you to learn the basics of Python programming.

The next step is to learn more about Python! You should have expected that coming.

Kidding aside, with the current knowledge you have in Python programming, you can make any programs like that with ease. But of course, there are still lots of things you need to learn about the language such as loops, classes, and etcetera.

Finally, if you enjoyed this book, please take the time to share your thoughts and post a review on Amazon. We do our best to reach out to readers and provide the best value we can. Your positive review will help us achieve that. It'd be greatly appreciated!

Thank you and good luck!

Book 2
JavaScript Professional Programming Made Easy

By Sam Key

Expert JavaScripts Programming Language Success in a Day for Any Computer User!

Table Of Contents

Introduction

I want to thank you and congratulate you for purchasing the book, "Professional JavaScript Programming Made Easy: Expert JavaScripts Programming Language Success In A Day for Any Computer User!"

This book contains proven steps and strategies on how to code JavaScript from scratch.

This book will give you a solid idea on how JavaScript works and how it can be applied to your web pages. This is an ideal book that every beginner should read. However, it is required that you already know HTML and CSS.

Familiarity with other programming languages such as Java, Visual Basic, and C is a plus since it will make it easier for you to learn and understand the concepts behind the processes involved in coding JavaScript.

Every explanation in the book will be accompanied by an example. Those examples will be shown in Courier New font; in case that font is not available, it will be shown in a monospaced generic family font instead.

To learn and code JavaScript, all you need is a text editing tool such as Notepad in Windows or TextEdit in Macintosh computers. However, it is recommend that you use a source code editor or a text editing tool with syntax highlighting that supports HTML, CSS, and JavaScript languages to speed up your learning and reduce the typos you will make.

One of the best and free source code editor tools you can get from the internet is Notepad++. It will be discussed in the last chapter of the book.

Thanks again for purchasing this book, I hope you enjoy it!

Chapter 1: Introduction to JavaScript

JavaScript is a scripting or programming language that is mainly used for web pages. Almost all websites use it to provide their visitors a richer browsing experience. Compared to coding HTML, JavaScript is real programming.

It is safe to say that JavaScript is the most popular and most widely used programming language in the world. JavaScript is easy to learn, and that is why web developers or even hobbyists can use it after a few days of studying it.

Unlike other programming languages, JavaScript is easy to learn and apply practically. The programs or scripts created from JavaScript are used by millions of people – even though they do not know they are already using them.

JavaScript can turn your old HTML files, which are static, into dynamic. You can embed JavaScript into your files for you to deliver web pages with dynamic content and appearance.

To embed JavaScript to your HTML file, you must enclose your script inside script HTML tags (<script></script>). Commonly, you should place the script tags inside the head HTML tags (<head></head>). However, there will be times that you might want or need to place them inside your page's body (<body></body>).

On the other hand, JavaScript can be placed in an external file and linked on a web page to work. It will be considered to be a part of the HTML file being parsed by the browser once it is linked.

Client and Server Side Scripting

In web development, JavaScript is termed as a client side scripting language. All the scripts that you write in JavaScript are executed on the client side, which is your or your visitors' browser.

On the other hand, PHP and ASP are server side scripting languages. As you might have guessed, the scripts or programs created using those two are executed on the server and their results are usually sent to the client.

The two complete the concept of DHTML (Dynamic HTML). When you use client and server side scripting, your pages will become more dynamic and interactive. With them, you can create social media websites, online games, and even your own search engine. And those statements are not exaggerated. You are truly a few steps away from greatness once you master JavaScript and a server side scripting language.

However, take note that learning client side scripting is a prerequisite before learning server side scripting. After all, most of the functions and features that you will create using server side scripting will require or need the support of client side scripting. Also, client side scripting is a good introduction to programming for web developers who have no experience or even any idea on how programming works.

Before you start learning and applying JavaScript to your web documents, you should learn and master HTML and CSS. In JavaScript, you will be mostly dealing with HTML elements, so it is a requirement that you know about HTML elements and attributes.

Alternatively, if you want to use JavaScript to perform advanced styling on your document such as animations and dynamic layouts, then you should have a solid background on CSS.

To give you a short summary of the relationship between HTML, CSS, and JavaScript, take note of these pointers:

- HTML is used to define the content and elements of your web page.
- CSS is used to specify or precisely define the appearance and layout of your web page.
- JavaScript is used to create functionalities in your web page. It can also be used to define content like HTML and define appearances like CSS.

With JavaScript, you can fully control everything on your web page. You can change an HTML element's content. For example, you can change the text content of a paragraph element with JavaScript.

You can also change the value of one of the attributes of an HTML element. For example, you can change the HREF attribute of a link you inserted on your document.

And lastly, you can change the CSS or styling values of an HTML element. For example, you can change the font-weight of one of your headers in your web document with JavaScript, too.

Also, with JavaScript, you have full control on when it will be applied, unlike CSS. You can run your scripts before the page loads, while the page is loading, after the page loaded, and while your user browses the page.

On the other hand, you can make those changes automatic or triggered by the visitor. You can add other factors such as time of the day, specific user actions, or user browsing behavior to trigger those changes or functions.

Chapter 2: HTML DOM and Assigning Values

How can JavaScript do all of that? It can do all of that because it takes advantage of the HTML DOM or Document Object Model. JavaScript can access, modify, and remove any HTML element together with its properties by using HTML DOM.

Assigning Attribute Values with JavaScript

With CSS, you have dealt with selectors. By using the right selector, you can change the CSS style of a specific element, group or class of elements, group of similar elements, handpicked elements, or all of the elements in your page. By this point, you must already know how id's and classes works.

JavaScript almost works like that, too. To change the content of an element, value of an element's property or attribute, or style of an element, you will need to select them first and assign a value. Below is an example of using JavaScript to change a paragraph element's (which has a value of "testparagraph" for its id attribute) font size:

```
<head>
<script>
document.getElementById("testparagraph" ).style.fontSize = "17px";
</script>
</head>
<body>
<p id='testparagraph' >This a paragraph. This is another sentence. This is the last sentence.</p>
</body>
```

The previous line's equivalent to CSS is:

```
#testparagraph {font-size: 17px;}
```

They have different syntax, but they will have the same result. In the CSS example, the paragraph with the "testparagraph" id was selected by placing a pound sign and typing the id value.

In JavaScript, "testparagraph" was selected using DOM. If you will translate the example JavaScript line to plain English, the line says to the browser that the line of code pertains to something or will do something within the document, which is your webpage.

Then the next part tells the browser that you are looking for a certain element that has a value of "testparagraph" on its id attribute. The next part tells the browser that you will do something to the style attribute of the "testparagraph" element. And the last part tells the browser that you will assign a value on the fontSize within the element's style attribute.

In JavaScript, the equals sign (=) means that you will assign a value to the variable or property on its left. And the value that you will assign on the variable or property is on the right.

On the example, you will assign the value "17px" to the fontSize style attribute of the element "testparagraph" that is located within your HTML document. The semicolon at the end tells the browser that it is the end of the line for that code, and it should parse the next line for it to execute.

Browser Parsing Behavior

By default, that previous JavaScript example will not work. The reason is that browsers read and execute HTML documents line by line – from the starting tag of the html tag, the browser will perform scripts, apply CSS values, place the HTML elements, place their specific contents, etcetera, until the browser reach the closing html tag.

In the example, the line asks the browser for an element that has the value "testparagraph" in its id attribute in the document. Unfortunately, the browser has not reached the body of the document where the definition of the element "testparagraph" resides.

Because of that, the browser will return an error saying that there is no element that has that attribute. You cannot assign a value for the attribute font size style to a nonexistent or null object. Hence, when the browser reaches the definition of the element "testparagraph", its font size will not be changed to the value you have set in the JavaScript code.

The solution to that is simple: you can place the script after the part where the element "testparagraph" was defined, and that is any location after the closing paragraph of the element "testparagraph".

Chapter 3: JavaScript Statements

In the last part of the previous chapter, the book loosely discussed about how browsers read HTML files and JavaScript lines and how you can assign values to an attribute. This chapter will supplement you with further discussions about that and JavaScript statements.

To construct a program using a programming language, you will need to write lines of codes. Those lines of codes are called statements. A statement is a line of code that contains an instruction for the computer to execute. In JavaScript, the one that executes the code is your internet browser.

Statements in JavaScript might contain the following: Keywords, Expressions, Operators, Comments, and Values. Below are sample lines of JavaScript that this chapter will dissect; this is done so that you will know the parts that comprise JavaScript statements:

```
var x; // This is a comment line.
var y; // To create one, you must place two forward slashes.
var z; // Comment lines are ignored by the browser.
x = 1 + 1; // So you can place them before or after a statement.
y = "Hello World." // And it will not affect the syntax.
z = 10 // But do not put them in the middle of a statement.
```

Keywords

In the example, the word var is a keyword. Typically, keywords are reserved words that you cannot use in your program except when you need to use their purpose. In the sample statements, the keyword var tells the browser to create a variable named x. Variables will be discussed later.

Expressions

On the other hand, 1 + 1 is an expression and the + and = sign are examples of operators. Expressions, in computer programming, are combinations of operators, values, constants, and variables that will be interpreted by the computer to produce a result. In x = 1 + 1, the browser will compute or evaluate that expression and return a value of 2. Expressions are not limited to arithmetic operations in JavaScript. Expressions can be in form of Boolean comparison, string operations, and etcetera.

Values

There are two values types that you will see and use in JavaScript. The first type is fixed or literal values; the second type is variables.

Literal Values

Numbers, Strings (text enclosed in single or double quotes), and even Expressions are literal values. In the example, the parts "Hello World" (string), 10 (number), and 1 + 1 (expression) are literal values.

Variables

On the other hand, variables are data containers. Variables can contain literal values such as strings, numbers, arrays, expressions, and even objects.

To use or create one, you must name it or create an identifier for it. Identifiers are combinations of letters, underscores, and dollar signs and must not be the same with any keywords or reserved words in JavaScript.

However, take note that identifiers must start with a letter, an underscore, or a dollar sign only. Starting with a number will return an error, and including symbols other than underscores and dollar signs will not be accepted by JavaScript.

Local Variable and Global Variables

There are two types of variables in JavaScript. The first one is local and the second one is global. The type of variable depends on where it was declared. The difference between them is how they are handled in the script.

Variables that are declared outside of functions will become a global variable. And variables that are declared inside functions will become a local variable.

Global variables will stay on the memory until the web page is closed. It can be referenced and used anywhere in the script. On the other hand, local variables will only stay on the memory until the browser finishes executing the function where the variable was declared. It can be only referenced and used by the function where it was declared. Functions will be discussed later in this book.

In the sample JavaScript statements, the letters x, y, and z are global variables.

To create a variable in JavaScript, you must use the var keyword – just like in the previous example. To assign values to them, you can use the equal operator.

Operators

There are multiple of operators that you can use in JavaScript. And it can be categorized into the following:

- Arithmetic
- Assignment
- String
- Comparison
- Logical
- Conditional

- Bitwise
- Typeof
- Delete Unary +

Only the first four types of operators are mostly the ones that you will frequently use during your early days of JavaScript programming: Arithmetic, Assignment, String, and Comparison. The remaining operators are typically used for advanced projects and might be confusing for beginners.

On the other hand, take note that some of the operator symbols may serve two purposes or more. For example, the + sign can be used as an arithmetic, string, or unary + operator depending on the condition or your goal.

Comments

You might already have an idea on what comments are. As mentioned before, they are ignored by browsers, and their only function is to serve as reminders or notes for you – just like the comments in HTML. You can create a new line of comment by using two forward slashes. If you want to create a block of comment, start it with /* and end it with */.

Chapter 4: JavaScript's Basic Syntax

For the browser to execute a JavaScript statement, the statement must follow the correct syntax and must only have one instruction (this may vary depending the code).

Just a small mistake in the syntax will make the computer do something different from what you want to happen or it might not do nothing and return an error.

If you have a large block of code and one of the statements gets an error, the browser will not execute the lines that follow the statement that generated an error.

Due to that, it is important that you always check your code and avoid creating mistakes to make sure that you will achieve the things you want to happen with JavaScript.

JavaScript Syntax

JavaScript, just like other computer languages, follow syntax. In computer programming, syntax is a set of rules that you must follow when writing codes.

One of the syntax rules in JavaScript is to terminate each statement with a colon. It is like placing a dot in every sentence you make.

This rule is flexible due to ASI (Automatic Semicolon Inserting). Even if you do not place a semicolon at the end of your statement, once you start a new line, the previous line will be considered as a complete statement – as if it has a semicolon at the end. However, not placing semicolons is bad practice since it might produce bugs and errors.

Another rule is to make sure that you close brackets, parentheses, and quotations in your code. For example, leaving a dangling curly brace will result in an error. And with quotation marks, if you started with a single quote, end it with a single quote. If you start with a double quote, end with a double quote.

Take note that JavaScript is a case-sensitive language. Unlike HTML wherein you can use lower, upper, and mixed case on tags and attributes, JavaScript will return an error once you use the wrong case for a method or variable. For example, changing the capitalization of the letter b in the getElementById will result to an error.

Never create variables that have the similar name with keywords or reserved words. Also, always declare variables. If you do not explicitly declare them and use them on your statements, you might get unexpected results or a reference error. For example:

```
var y;
var z;
```

```
y = 1;
z = 1 + x;
```

Once your browser reads the last line, no value will be assigned to z because the browser will return a reference error.

That is just a few of the rules in JavaScript's syntax. Some methods and keywords follow certain syntax. Remember them to prevent yourself from the hassle of unneeded debugging.

Chapter 5: Functions and Events

You already know by now what statements are and how to write statements in accordance to JavaScript's syntax rules. You also know how to assign values to an HTML element's attribute by using JavaScript. In this chapter, you will know how to create functions or methods.

A function is a block of statements that you can call or invoke anytime to execute. In other programming languages, functions are called subroutines, methods, or procedures. The statements inside a function will not be immediately executed when the browser parses the HTML document. It will only run or be executed if it is called or invoked.

Purposes of Functions

What are the purposes of functions? First, it allows you to control when to execute a block of statements as explained previously.

Second, it allows you to create 'mini' programs in your script. For example, if you want to make a paragraph to be centered align, to have a heavier font, and to have a bigger font size when you click the paragraph, you can create a function for that goal and capture an event that will trigger that function once you click on the paragraph.

Third, creating functions is a good way to separate lengthy blocks of statements into smaller chunks. Maintaining and debugging your script will be much easier with functions.

Fourth, it can effectively lessen redundancy in your script. Instead of writing the same sequence of statements repeatedly in your script, you can just create a function, and just call it again when you need the browser to execute the statements within it once more.

Creating Functions

To create a function, you will need to use the keyword function. When you create a function you must follow a simple syntax. Below is an example of a function:

```
function MakeBolderAndBigger(elementID) {
document.getElementById(elementID).style.fontSize = "20px";
document.getElementById(elementID).style.fontWeight = "20px";
}
```

In the example, the keyword function was followed with MakeBolderAndBigger. That part is the function's name. Naming a function has the same rules with naming a variable identifier.

After the function's name, there is elementID which is enclosed in parentheses. That part of the function is called a parameter. You can place as many parameters that you want or none at all. If you place multiple parameters, you must separate them with a comma and a space. If you are not going to use parameters, just leave it blank but never forget to place the parentheses.

A parameter stores that value or the function arguments that was placed on it when the function is invoked. That parameter will act as local variable in the function. This part will be discussed further later.

Then, after the parameter, you will see a curly brace. And after the statements, there is another curly brace.

The first brace act as a sign that tells the browsers that any statements following it is a code block for the function. The second brace tells the browsers that the code block is finished, and any line of code after it is not related to the function. Those are the rules you need to follow when creating a function.

Invoking Functions

There are two common ways to invoke a function. First, you can invoke it within your script. Second, you can invoke it by placing and triggering event handlers.

Invoke within Code

The first method of invoking functions is easy. All you need to do is to type the name of the function, and fill in the arguments that the function's parameters require. To invoke the example function using the first method, you can simply type this:

MakeBolderAndBigger("testparagraph");
Once your browser reads that, it will process the function. Since you have placed "testparagraph" as the argument for the parameter elementID, elementID will have a value of "testparagraph". It will now act as a variable.

When the browser executes the first statement in the function, which is document.getElementById(elementID).style.fontSize = "20px";, it will select the element "testparagraph" and change its font size value to 20px.

On the other hand, you can actually provide no argument for function parameters. If you do this instead:

MakeBolderAndBigger();
The browser will execute the function. However, since you did not store any value to the parameter, the parameter elementID will be undefined and will have the value undefined.

Because of that, when the first statement tries to look for the element with the id attribute of elementID, which has the value of undefined, it will return an error.

Once the browser finishes executing the function, it will return on reading the next line of code after the function invocation. For example:

MakeBolderAndBigger("testparagraph");

```
document.getElementById("testparagraph").style.color = "blue";
```

After the browser finishes executing the function MakeBolderAndBigger, it will proceed on executing the next statement below and make the font color of "testparagraph" to blue. The example above is the same as coding:

```
document.getElementById("testparagraph" ).style.fontSize = "20px";
document.getElementById("testparagraph" ).style.fontWeight = "20px";
document.getElementById("testparagraph" ).style.color = "blue";
```

Invoke with Events

Every action that a user does in a web page and every action that the browser performs are considered events. A few of those events are:

- When the page finishes loading
- When a user or script changes the content of a text field
- When a user click a button or an HTML element
- When a user presses on a keyboard key

To invoke a function when an event happens, you must tell the browser by placing some piece of codes in your page's HTML. Below is an example:

```
<button onClick='MakeBolderAndBigger("testparagraph");' >Invoke Function</button>
```

When a user clicks on that button element, it will trigger the function MakeBolderAndBigger. The syntax for that is simple. Just insert the event inside the opening tag of an HTML element that has the event that you want to capture, place an equal sign, place the function that you want to execute together with the arguments you need to place on it, and then enclose the function in quotes.

By the way, be wary of quotes. If you used a single quote to enclose the function, then use double quotes to enclose the values on your arguments. Just think of it as if you are assigning values on an element's style attribute in HTML. Also, as best practice, never forget to place a semicolon at the end.

As a reference, below are some of the events that you can use in HTML and JavaScript:

- onClick – triggers when the user clicks on the HTML element
- onMouseOver – triggers when the user hovers on the HTML element
- onMouseOut – triggers when the user's mouse pointers move out from the element's display
- onKeyDown – triggers when the user presses a keyboard key
- onChange – triggers when the user changes the content of a text field
- onLoad – triggers when the browser is done loading the body, images, frames, and other scripts

Chapter 6: Debugging, Text Editing Tool, and References

In modern browsers, most of JavaScript errors are handled automatically and ignored to prevent browsing disruption. So when testing your scripts when opening your HTML files on a browser, it is difficult to spot errors and debug.

Web Developer Consoles on Browsers

Fortunately, a few of those browsers have built-in developer consoles where you can monitor errors and the resources that your page generates and uses. One of those browsers that have this functionality is Google Chrome. To access its developer console, you can press F12 on your keyboard while a page is open on it.

Pressing the key will open the developer tools panel within Chrome, and you can click on the Console tab to monitor the errors that your page generates. Aside from monitoring errors, you can use it to test statements, check the values of your variables, call functions, etc.

Text Editing Tool with Syntax Highlighting

You can get away with a few problems when writing HTML and CSS on typical text editing tools like Notepad. However, with JavaScript coding, using those ordinary tools is a challenge. Unlike the two, JavaScript has a strict and vast syntax. Just one typo in your script and you will start hunting bugs after you test the statements you wrote. After all, it is a programming language unlike HTML which is a markup language.

To make your life easier, it is best that you use a text editing tool with syntax highlighting when coding JavaScript. One of the best tools out there on the Web is Notepad++. It is free and it is as lightweight (in terms of resource usage) and as simple as Notepad.

The syntax highlighting will help you spot missing brackets and quotation marks. It will also prevent you from using keywords as variables since keywords are automatically highlighted in a different color, which will help you realize sooner that they are identifiers you cannot use for variables.

References

As of now, you have only learned the basics of how to code JavaScript. You might have been itching to change the values of other attributes in your HTML code, but you do not know the HTML DOM to use. On the other hand, you might be interested on knowing the other operators that you can use in your script.

The book has omitted most of them since it focused more on the coding process in JavaScript. Thankfully, you can just look up those values and operators on the net. To give you a head start, this a link to the JavaScript reference list made by the developers in the Mozilla Foundation: https://developer.mozilla.org/en-US/docs/Web/JavaScript/Reference.

Conclusion

Thank you again for purchasing this book!

I hope this book was able to help you to learn the basics of coding with JavaScript.

The next step is to:

Master the HTML DOM.

Become familiar with other keywords and their usage.

Finally, if you enjoyed this book, please take the time to share your thoughts and post a review on Amazon. We do our best to reach out to readers and provide the best value we can. Your positive review will help us achieve that. It'd be greatly appreciated!

Thank you and good luck!

Check Out My Other Books

Below you'll find some of my other popular books that are popular on Amazon and Kindle as well. Simply click on the links below to check them out. Alternatively, you can visit my author page on Amazon to see other work done by me.

C Programming Success in a Day

Android Programming in a Day

C ++ Programming Success in a Day

C Programming Professional Made Easy

Python Programming in a Day

PHP Programming Professional Made Easy

HTML Professional Programming Made Easy

CSS Programming Professional Made Easy

Windows 8 Tips for Beginners

If the links do not work, for whatever reason, you can simply search for these titles on the Amazon website to find them.

www.ingramcontent.com/pod-product-compliance
Lightning Source LLC
Chambersburg PA
CBHW060931050326
40689CB00013B/3050
* 9 7 8 1 5 1 2 0 9 3 0 3 2 *